When the Bird Is Not a Human

When the Bird Is Not a Human
HR Hegnauer

SUBITO PRESS 2018

When the Bird Is Not a Human © HR Hegnauer, 2018
All rights reserved.

ISBN: 978-0-9988594-7-7

Cover collage, design & typesetting by HR Hegnauer
    www.hrhegnauer.com
Text typeset in Adobe Garamond Pro and My Underwood

Subito Press
Department of English
University of Colorado at Boulder
226 UCB
Boulder, CO 80309-0226
subitopress.org

Distributed by Small Press Distribution
1341 Seventh Street
Berkeley, California 94710
spdbooks.org

Generous funding for this publication has been provided by the Creative Writing Program in the Department of English and the Innovative Seed Grant Program at the University of Colorado at Boulder.

CONTENTS

The Characters
- 3 The Dog
- 4 The White-Crowned Sparrow
- 5 The Constellation

The Settings & The Scenes
- 9 The Yard
- 10 The Parking Space
- 11 The Porch
- 12 The Doorway
- 13 The Kitchen
- 14 The Dining Room
- 15 The Garbage
- 16 The Living Room
- 17 The Stairwell
- 18 The Hallway
- 19 The Bedroom
- 20 The Bed
- 22 The Sound
- 23 The Haunting
- 24 The Bathroom
- 25 The Baby
- 26 The Dark-haired Man
- 27 The Thought
- 28 The Time
- 29 The Ingestions
- 30 The Road
- 31 The Visions
- 32 The Skin

33 The Arms
34 The Gender
35 The Disaster
36 The Thought, Revisited
37 The Creek
38 The Message
39 The Lake
40 The Cloud
41 The Doorway, Revisited
42 The Kitchen, Revisited
43 The Plate
44 The Living Room, Revisited
45 The Red String
46 The Goose
47 The Window
48 The Living Room, Re-revisited
49 The Seen
50 The Onwards
51 The Bedroom, Revisited
52 The Bed, Revisited
53 The Baby, Revisited
54 The Living

The And

57 The And
58 The Tiger
59 The Moon

for Monette

THE CHARACTERS

The Dog

How the leashed did not say, *Hold me*
around the throat so that I cannot lick my own breathing.
How the leash took the blame from the leasher
and held that, too, before seeing that

the bone behind the black-tendoned engine is chewless
and turns wedded hands to metal stones
at the axis of probing junctions.

And after that. And seeing that.
The belly's blown out
in the wake of the dust
past the leash still strapped
to the barrel of the lungs.

How the leashed wanted to bark
naked as the dog is
with no more sounding
like *this second could be my*

first to not want
the nakedness of tendoned engines
with the hood ripped off and strewn
split down on the meadowed highway

mid-south, from destinations unknown
to sinewed reverse
and so, we're humming what these birds won't speak.

The White-Crowned Sparrow

I looked — didn't I
look,
look, look —
Yes. This is what I did.

Dear bird, dear fluttering one at my window,
I wanted to *see you*, but you have flocked.
And so I ask — but of no one in particular —
is there *providence in the fall of the sparrow?*
Yes, yes of course there is, says no one in particular.
And so as I am all of wanting, here is my call to this hamlet:
While you're gone, I will navigate my human limbs
along all the crevices of this house
and along the eaves of this attic,
and I will search out your nest.

Dear sparrow,
I cannot *see you*, and so I've placed my body
along the pathway where the mountain meets grassland,
and I listen for your thin, sweet whistle.

The phenomenon of dialect is the focus of my attention.
What does a two-second song pattern sound like?
It sounds like fluctuations. It sounds like
a striped crown —
like all of these syllables I cannot say,
this is what it sounds like to see a thing.

The Constellation

Innocuous was not the word.
Human was the word.

We put the human in the star space
not knowing that
the star space didn't want the human.

We were talking about it and I thought,
I think so.
Yes, I think so.

No, not that.

Yes, I would think so.
Wouldn't you?

THE SETTINGS

&

THE SCENES

The Yard

We projected our silent movie on
    the back of the house:
        The Celebration of Finished Things.

She watered the lawn — I mowed it.
Our astrology confirmed this.

The Parking Space

Let's make a garden,
    I said.
It'll be like Joni Mitchell in reverse,
    she said.

And it was.

The Porch

To rock on the swing and hear the wind chimes
is a heaven cut short.

The buzzing streetlight.

A cat named thunder.
A bird named flicker.
A fox unnamed.

The squirrel eats the pumpkin.

The Doorway

A friend and I try to guess
how many buttons we've ever pushed.
How many years are in a billions seconds?
This seems like a useful question, and so we both ask it.

Sometimes, I push more than one button at a time.
    I say to him.
Yes, I know. He says to me. *So do I.*

We enter through the kitchen, and there are two of them.
We enter through the side of the kitchen.
We enter from beneath the kitchen.
We enter through the mud room, and here is the kitchen.
There are pockmarks on the floor from stilettos.

The Kitchen

The Dining Room

She knew she tried to know this room
until she couldn't separate
her own colors from her sounds anymore
as if the colors
    somehow
        might have
            existed in shades of
    do's and don'ts.
All she wanted was a color past clear like not through
under the table
    that is as solid as the cup as the table.

The Garbage

And then a tiny man on horseback.
A shoe.
A saddle.

We took this garbage and we hung it
on the wall.

The dining room never looked so —.
What was that word again?
Must have been something from the kitchen.

The Living Room

And then all I could hear was, *We take our pleasures.*
And then I removed my eyes.

Couldn't look around the living room anymore.
Couldn't sit on the blue couch and look at the books.

So I put the room in a box.
I put the box on a truck on a road,
and then I put it in a bigger box.

I put my eyes in that bigger box, too,
and then I drove away.

I do not know what happened before noon.
I remember noon.

Before noon was a gap that was bigger than a space.
I know this because when I put the space in the gap,
there were still more gaps.

I pushed myself to sleep.
There was a dream about what it means to be one human.
This was not my dream, but it existed within my sleep.

This was how my dream thought: and-less-ly.

The Stairwell

To spill wooden sounds into the morning
like this place
    is the most accurate stair,
and that place
    is just full of lung space
until this stair follows that stair.

They've always been like this:
    these stairs.
One stepping upon another.
This is how we built them.

And this is how we'll weather them:
    I'll touch this lip
until it's smoothed itself over in an oiled way.
    You'll touch the next lip
just the same,
and when we compare the weather,
    I will close my eyes.

The Hallway

I fell asleep.
The light or no light.
What am I doing?

I am looking for the room,
    but the room does not exist.
So I built a door,
    painted it blue,
        surrounded it with bricks.

Still, the room does not exist.

The Bedroom

The vent blows warm air into this room
    until the night becomes its latest hour.
I listen until the air becomes confused with its sounds —
    the same way a word becomes demented once you've
looked at it for too long.

This is the part when I imagine that the air sounds
    are actually another human's breathing patterns.

And I think the air believes me.
I mean, I think the sounds believe me.
    Or at the very least,
        they're too confused to know the difference,
and that's become good enough for me.

The Bed

Just coming to the thought process:

How could an act fuck it up
until it began writing?

How could an act be anything but birth until it began writing
mother fucker, be anything but birth.

It was more than a word,
mother fucker,
— a baby entering a writing —
It was more than a word in the voice of a baby entering a writing.

To make a language in the voice of
— as in fuck you —
To make a language only a little less fucked up as in fuck you.

I was a conduit
only a little less fucked up.
I'm fucking kidding.

I was a conduit for my imagined imagination of a baby.
I'm fucking kidding.
I mean, you wanna fuck for my imagined imagination of a baby
brought into a suffering world?

I mean, you wanna fuck
and relive creation?

Brought into a suffering world and separated out to say

> *Relive creation.*
> *We came from water,*

and were separated out to say,
fuck you.
We came from water
coming from the thought process.

The Sound

It became animal,
      and it did this in a hurry.
There were no colors.

The Haunting

She walked in an elle-shaped pattern:
    A white night gown.
    Blood upon her cuffs.
I was not supposed to be here.
This much was clear.

I left the bedroom to enter the bedroom of another,
    but the haunts here were even greater.

When every light was a candle
and the wind was inside the room,
the darkness was as thick as bees.
Were you the one who left the gate open?
    No.
Well that's how all the bees got in.

The Bathroom

But was it a laceration?
Yes, it was a laceration.
I hung onto the brushes and the soap.

The Baby

After the last time we made love,
I gave birth to a still-born boy.
A dream in the bed of failure.
The dark-haired man is dead.

The Dark-Haired Man

I don't see him so much as dead as I see him as a shape-shifter.

That's what the thought looked like
    from the brown chair
        once the thought had been accurately revisited.

It looked like a sudden flash.
That is to say, it did not look like a path,
    but it looked like a destination,
    and somehow the thought knew
    that it could hold this contradiction,
        and somehow it did.

The Thought

I aim to intuit only thought from imagination.
Today is warm, but falling.

A dirty white shirt tucked beneath overalls
    tucked beneath laceless shoes.
Dirt stuck to candy stuck to a face.
A portrait of a child.

And from this slanting position, I know
    that what is odd is in no way common.
And what is common is a gaggle —
    a gaggle of children.
And the thought intuits the child.

The Time

It wasn't now.
    Shaky as it is — it wasn't.

The text muffled the birdsong until it became a new language.

What time is it?
    (I've already asked this question.)
A bustling of hands in a circular fashion.
A child fond of the intersection.

The Ingestions

I had one.
Then another.
    Repeat.
        Repeat.
           Repeat.
I cannot count this many stars anymore.

I have become my least favorite child in these times of counting being brought home by my most favorite animal.

Yes, this is a spectrum.
No, this is not a spectrum-based consciousness.

I am not the search party for the star gone dim.

The Road

A dead porcupine. A dead opossum.
Crow, coyote, elk, and armadillo.
The lovely disorientation of something good.

Life is like an unused bulldozer on the side of the road:
Sometimes you need to clear all bits of everything.
So you get in the driver's seat and turn the key
only to realize you're out of gas,

and that dead porcupine
was just a clump of grass.

The Visions

This is the dark room.
    These colors. These edges.
I went out wandering the road looking for conversation.
    And the road made noises, and the noises made colors again.

Darkness is a vision,
    said the visionary.

If I see you pushing a baby carriage, said the visionary's mother,
I'm going to kill you.

A sudden stab of the imagination,
    said the visionary.

But nothing was in this order, and nothing was orderly.
I looked through the neighbor's kitchen window,
but there wasn't any order there either.

Someone said the order was on sale,
but then someone sold the store.

Blindness is sweet for temporary voice:
a reflection in the window I never knew I saw.

The Skin

To worry about the quality of your skin
    is to worry about death.
I have been thinking about this for years now,
and every unfinished manuscript is a reflection upon
    the skinning and its acute irritations.

Bathe me in safflower oil and salt.
I am a stilled itch.

The Arms

A friend and I compare our man-arms.
He wins.
I am not a man.

The Gender

I once was a man.
    [I remember little.]

This is the gone now.
All is a goneness.
What is this material?
The nuances of such a light feathering in the
    [I don't remember.]

The gone now.
My body in the goneness.
    [Go in.]

Here now
Just now
See you
    Here is the passage:

The Disaster

I have imagined you in every disaster,
    she says to me.
In every great depression.

I can't remember how this thought came to be a good thing.
It became itself so naturally.

A paradise of reality.

The Thought, Revisited

Just thinking about stuff. What goes where…
  said the green couch to the blue couch.

Won't you come and sit beside me?

The answer was this:
  When spaceships fly.

```
The Creek
```

The honorable lights —
    I don't know how it got like this,
        but they were everywhere
        lighting everything —

Here now,
    just now,
        see you.
Little flashing bits.

Step number one:
    Stand here.
Step number two:
    Put the baby hair in the creek.

The Message

I have the confidence of a million fucking suns,
and here is what I want to say to you:

    I care for you in dear ways.

The Lake

To slow down the way the trees sway
    when the wind pushes the ember sounds:
Lake language: a mirror of what I want to give you.

But I can't give you a lake:
    A fantasy world —
    smoke in my eyes.

But I can give you my pattern language:
    Plaid laid upon a lichen-covered rock —
    and it does exist.

I put myself into this night and say
    Collect me.
    Collect this cloud within my mouth.

The Cloud

Looks like a pig riding atop a dove.

We live here now:
    The garment-making factory.
The neighbors got the meat-packing building.
    They live there without the meat.

Like seeing brown instead of red
    but knowing they're both still colors,
        we were eating the clouds
            right out of the cloud soup out of our bowls.

The Doorway, Revisited

To mourn is to mourn the loss of the present
    inside of the future.

Are these beats melodic?
    This is the question.
Was I the first to sign the threshold?
    This is the answer.

    When the doorway is no longer white,
    and every room is a doorway,
    and every doorway is a saint,
Go in.

The Kitchen, Revisited

The first time,
    I could not speak of it,
    so I kept the silence.

The second time,
    I put my pot in your skillet,
    and you said, *close the kitchen.*

```
The Plate
```

Her ancestors ate from this plate.
They ate the doves and the hogs and pain perdu, too.
Their cookbook rests upon my earl grey tea.
A mutual offer.

When I sip my tea and look at the plate,
I mutter a prayer to the fancy lady in the white dress:
    Dear Patron Saint of the Aviators,
        Let this plate be a plate in flight.
    Amen.

The Living Room, Revisited

The diamonds were made from bottles,
and she got to name every feather on every bird.

That's what the room looked like
    from the blue couch
        once the room had accurately been revisited.
It looked like feet and hands.

That is to say, it looked like
    a human awake and a human asleep
at the same time, and once these two humans saw this,
they knew they were seeing themselves
    from inside of the visitation,
and they saw this during the moment of sound.

The Red String

When she was wrapped around the waste in red string;
when she was washed in rose and jasmine;
when she read out loud about how to make an animal family;
her mother said,
    So you're just going to float all this out there then?
    Just put all this in the water?

Yes.

She realized then that she had never felt so close to *and*
    as in this second
        and as in the next.

The Goose

To float upon this thin wind with heavy ease—
I watch these birds from not so far away,
and envy their awkward repetitions.

If I could make my body blend, I would.
I'd go inside the asters and the four o'clocks
    and all the wild grasses,
and make a little bed for blending bodies.

If ever true were these words, *hope is a waking dream*,
I'd know them upon my floating.

I thought your arm was my arm.
It is.

I am the gatherer of sun beneath the shadows of a flight
that is at once arbitrary and meaningful,
and I am full of gathering.

What is an arbitrary pattern?
This place of sight.

```
The Window
```

Breathtaking is the only thing I can read.
I mean this literally.

The Living Room, Re-revisited

Here is a shuffle.
Here is a lift.
A crumple of newspaper.
This is how a rotation moves—
The same way a feather moves
    when it hangs from the ventilation.

To see the living room not as a mirrored circle,
    but as one that encompasses a mirrored circle,
    you must polish the mirror and look in it.
Look in it while sitting on the blue couch.

This is when the books look back at you through the mirror.
    They look at you with the confidence of a million fucking suns.
    They look at you with the humility of every story ever heard.

In return, the attempt is to see.
This is the this is: the attempt at seeing.

The Seen

Like the dog who will not come only because he is unable,
    not because he lacks desire,
The seen has never been seen.

There were all these people in the bottom one:
    Excuse me, excuse me.
    Yes?

We mumbled shapes towards one another,
    and they looked like desires.

`The Onwards`

When the little boy tells me his name is Lucy Window;
when Bobbie tells me she wants to drink wine
    if ever in hospice;
when Selah says, *lets turn purple bubbles.*
I say, *definitely.*
She says, *then every color.*
This is when I forget that we're living
    in the strangest world on earth.

The Bedroom, Revisited

Lessons in rituals in glamour:
    blue water atop the dresser,
    a window pane above the bed,
    feathers in one corner,
    and a rocking chair in the other.

I've never had a proper bedroom before,
    she says to me.
For mother and father,
    I read out loud.

A carving from someone else's ancestors.

The Bed, Revisited

I push my toes against the frame to grace momentum.
I push my forearm into the pillow to hold my body in sight.
    And the room smells like sex.
    And the world smells like sex.
    And I love this.
She puts her voice inside my ear.
I put my body inside our body's lives.

The Baby, Revisited

After the first time we made love,
I dreamt I was reading a story,
    and in the middle of the story,
I gave birth to a blonde-haired boy.

A dream in the bed of the revisitation.

I had never seen his face before this night —
    his vivid eyes.
He spoke to me in the way feathers speak —
    in wisps.

Trust me, for I cannot translate this.

The Living

If I am already dead,
    and this is my onwards,
then I am going to live it.
This is the meaning of *and*.

THE AND

The And,

I want to archive this.
The time is now 2:17 AM in the great state of Colorado, and this is an archive on *and*.

The Tiger

A recipe from the Old Testament:

Begin with breathing —
It's easy enough to forget,
    and this is not the space for forgetting.

Add the characters —
    The red-headed tiger knows the slab.
    The dog knows the stranger's humanity.
    The sparrow knows the sun.

Add the settings —
    This forest knows the trick-knee of the mind
        the same way time manufactures eternity.
    That is to say,
        it suffers its fools in the garden.

Scene 1:
    Stir.
    Swallow.
    Commence.

The Moon

The first time I saw it, it was in my hands. I wanted to look at it, but it faced away from me, and I realized then that to hold it without seeing it is an offense to the vision of it.

It knows no name. It moats its own island. It makes me forget the temperature of my own hands.

I raise it. I lower it. It asks me to count, and so I count. I began counting just like how a normal counter would. 1, 2, 3, and so on until I had reached to where I had raised it. Then I began counting quite unlike how a normal counter would. 300, 299, 298, and so forth. I just kept doing this — the raising and lowering of numbers.

When we looked at one another, we knew it was time to stop. All that chatter in the numbers, and it couldn't even hear it. It saw us before we saw it, and I think it must have seen us for some time now. But once we looked, we couldn't stop seeing it.

Notes

The White-Crowned Sparrow
"See you" is a phrase from Akilah Oliver's poem "an arriving guard of angels, thusly coming to greet" in the book *A Toast in the House of Friends* (Coffee House Press, 2009). "Providence in the fall of the sparrow" is a line from William Shakespeare's *Hamlet*.

The Dining Room
"Do's and don'ts" is a line from and reference to the song "Do's & Don'ts" (featuring Gruff Rhys) on the album *Blue Eyed in the Red Room* by Boom Bip (Lex Records, 2005). This album was used as a soundtrack while writing this manuscript.

The Garbage
The first stanza is a found-poem from a piece of trash. It looked to have been written by a young child. "Saddle" was originally spelled "sadl."

The Living Room
"We take our pleasures," is a line from *Essay on Ash*, a film by Ed Bowes, script by Laird Hunt (Walsung Compang).

The Sound
"There were no colors." is a line from *Essay on Ash*, a film by Ed Bowes, script by Laird Hunt (Walsung Compang).

The Ingestions
The line "I am not the search party for the star gone dim" is a reference to "There is no search party for a star gone dim" which is a line by Clouddead in the song "The Keen Teen Skip" on the album *Ten* (Mush Records, 2004).

The Gender
"See you" is a phrase from Akilah Oliver's poem "an arriving guard of angels, thusly coming to greet" in the book *A Toast in the House of Friends* (Coffee House Press, 2009).

The Creek
"See you" is a phrase from Akilah Oliver's poem "an arriving guard of angels, thusly coming to greet" in the book *A Toast in the House of Friends* (Coffee House Press, 2009).

The Goose
"Hope is a waking dream" is a quote from Aristotle.

The Tiger
Bobbie Louise Hawkins talked about the "trick knee of the mind" during her Naropa University Summer Writing Program reading on July 26, 2013. She said that "being a natural fool is like having a trick knee of the mind." She was talking about the book she was currently writing, which had a working title of *Gossip*, and was making a reference to Charles Olson.

The Moon
This poem was written in response to Joan Dickinson's performance art piece "The Dream of the Owl Sisters" and for her book on the project. The performance took place on the Platte River in Denver, Colorado on October 18, 2013.

Acknowledgments

Thank you to the editors who published some of these poems in the following places: *A Poetic Inventory of Rocky Mountain National Park*, *Aufgabe*, *Bombay Gin*, *Bone Bouquet*, *Denver Poetry Map*, *Dreginald*, *Puerto del Sol*, and *The Dream of the Owl Sisters*.

Thank you to Subito Press for bringing this book into the world. Thank you to everyone who has read and listened to these poems over the years. I am especially appreciative to Selah Saterstrom, Anne Waldman, Ed Bowes, Bobbie Louise Hawkins, Serena Chopra, Jennifer Denrow, Sarah Schantz, Mathias Svalina, and Joan Dickinson for reading and listening to numerous variations of these poems. Thank you to my family for your constant support and encouragement. This book is for Monette. May you always believe in the imagination's ability to re-imagine.

Subito Press Titles

2008
- *Little Red Riding Hood Missed the Bus* by Kristin Abraham
- *With One's Own Eyes: Sherwood Anderson's Realities* by Sherwood Anderson
  Edited and with an Introduction by Welford D. Taylor
- *Dear Professor, Do You Live in a Vacuum?* by Nin Andrews
- *My Untimely Death* by Adam Peterson

2009
- *Self-Titled Debut* by Andrew Farkas
- *F-Stein* by L.J. Moore

2010
- *Moon Is Cotton & She Laugh All Night* by Tracy Debrincat
- *Song & Glass* by Stan Mir
- *Bartleby, the Sportscaster* by Ted Pelton

2011
- *Man Years* by Sandra Doller
- *The Body, The Rooms* by Andy Frazee
- *Death-in-a-Box* by Alta Ifland

2012
- *We Have With Us Your Sky* by Melanie Hubbard
- *Vs. Death Noises* by Marcus Pactor
- *The Explosions* by Mathias Svalina

2013
- *Because I Am the Sea I Want to Be the Shore* by Renée Ashley
- *Domestic Disturbances* by Peter Grandbois
- *The Cucumber King of Kėdainiai* by Wendell Mayo

2014
As We Know by Amaranth Borsuk & Andy Finch
Liner Notes by James Brubaker
Letters & Buildings by Thomas Hummel

2016
Sometimes We Walk With Our Nails Out by Sarah Bartlett
Someone Took They Tongues. by Douglas Kearney
New Animals by Nick Francis Potter
To Think of Her Writing Awash in Light by Linda Russo

2017
Dear Enemy, by Jessica Alexander
Camera by Maxine Chernoff
A Forest Almost by Liz Countryman
Sam's Teeth by Patrick Culliton
He Always Still Tastes Like Dynamite by Trevor Dodge
Genevieves by Henry Hoke
Confessional Sci-fi: A Primer by Kirsten Kaschock
Anti-Face by Michael Nicoloff

2018
Your Love Alone is Not Enough by Richard Froude
Our Colony Beyond the City of Ruins: Stories by Janalyn Guo
When the Bird Is Not a Human by HR Hegnauer
ever really hear it by Soham Patel

ABOUT SUBITO PRESS

Subito Press is a non-profit literary publisher based in the Creative Writing Program of the Department of English at the University of Colorado at Boulder. Subito Press encourages and supports work that challenges already-accepted literary modes and devices.

www.ingramcontent.com/pod-product-compliance
Lightning Source LLC
Chambersburg PA
CBHW062120080426
42734CB00012B/2931